WONDERS and SURPRISES

Also by Phyllis McGinley

WONDERS
and
SURPRISES

A Collection of Poems
chosen by

PHYLLIS McGINLEY

J. B. Lippincott Company

PHILADELPHIA   NEW YORK

ACKNOWLEDGMENTS

For the right to reprint the copyrighted poems in this volume, the editor is indebted to the following poets, their families, agents, and publishers:

The Bodley Head Ltd. for "George III" from *Biography for Beginners* by E. C. Bentley.

Brandt & Brandt for "Nightmare Number Three" from *Selected Works of Stephen Vincent Benét*, Holt, Rinehart and Winston, Inc., copyright, 1940, by Stephen Vincent Benét; and "1936" from *Burning City* by Stephen Vincent Benét, published by Holt, Rinehart and Winston, Inc., copyright, 1936, by Stephen Vincent Benét, copyright renewed © 1964, by Thomas C. Benét, Stephanie B. Mahin, and Rachel Benét Lewis.

Elizabeth Coatsworth for her poem, "Song for Snow."

Curtis Brown, Ltd. for "The Buses Headed for Scranton" by Ogden Nash, copyright © 1956 by Ogden Nash, originally published in The New Yorker Magazine.

The John Day Company, Inc. for "Fife Tune" from *Selected Verse* by John Manifold, copyright 1946 by The John Day Co., Inc.

J. M. Dent & Sons Ltd. for "The Hand That Signed the Paper" from *Collected Poems* by Dylan Thomas, on behalf of the Trustees for the Copyrights of the late Dylan Thomas.

The Dial Press Inc. for "Spring" and "Song of the Pop-Bottlers"

For my children and theirs

Foreword

THIS IS A COLLECTION of poetry which, I hope, will give you pleasure.

I hope it will surprise you, interest you, even make you want to write a verse or two of your own. For poetry is the most ancient form of writing there is, and the most natural. Even before writing was invented, old bards were stringing their lyres and entertaining with poetry both the peasant in his cottage and the king in his castle. It is the way stories got told and history recorded.

There is not much history in this collection, unless you call the ballads history, which in a way they are—folk history. But there are stories and there is magic and there are comments on people and places and human nature. There is also —or so I trust—the delight of recognition. You ought to be able to say to yourself, when you have finished reading some verse or other, "Yes, yes. That is exactly the way things *are*." For there are many definitions of poetry but the best one I know is this: Poetry is what cannot be said so well in prose.

Everybody won't like all these poems. But I think everyone will enjoy at least a few of them. If you like mystery, there is mystery in the first section for you: magic and nightmares and incantations. If you are feeling romantic, there are romantic poems, and not sloppy ones, either. If you like animals, there are verses about dogs and bats and seals and even snails. And there are some marvelous curses. For poetry is chiefly emotion, and anger is as strong an emotion as love. In the section called "The Poison Pen," a number of poets have cursed war, evil, and their enemies. If ever you, yourself, feel in a rage over injustice or a wrong someone has done you, try writing out those feelings and notice how your spirits are relieved.

For that is what poetry ought to do for both you and the writer—relieve you of an excess of joy or sorrow or anger or surprise. Poetry is comment on the world by people who see that world more clearly than other people and are moved by it. They notice the changing of the year and write down their image of that change so that you, too, will notice things better than you did before. They express their wonder, their delight, their astonishment at the strangeness of this planet; and that wonder and that astonishment ought to carry over to you.

Except in the section called "Simple Nonsense," I have drawn no line between poetry which is written out of seriousness and that which was set down to amuse. Just as short stories or novels are still novels or short stories whether they are sad or funny, so poetry is still poetry no matter which emotion it arouses.

Read it the same way—with a mind open to both amusement and seriousness. And after you have read it, why not try your own hand at some form of this most honorable and natural art?

Contents

THE ANIMAL KINGDOM

LOVE AND KISSES

GENTLEMEN AND LADIES

THE POISON PEN

TRUMPET SOUNDS

FAR-OFF PLACES

THE CHANGING YEAR

RELATIVELY SPEAKING

STRANGENESSES

ECHO

'Who called?' I said, and the words
    Through the whispering glades,
Hither, thither, baffled the birds—
    'Who called? Who called?'

The leafy boughs on high
    Hissed in the sun;
The dark air carried my cry
    Faintingly on:

Eyes in the green, in the shade,
    In the motionless brake,
Voices that said what I said,
    For mockery's sake:

'Who cares?' I bawled through my tears;
    The wind fell low:
In the silence, 'Who cares? Who cares?'
    Wailed to and fro.

Walter de la Mare

NIGHTMARE NUMBER THREE

We had expected everything but revolt
And I kind of wonder myself when they started thinking—
But there's no dice in that now.

                      I've heard fellows say
They must have planned it for years and maybe they did.
Looking back, you can find little incidents here and there.
Like the concrete-mixer in Jersey eating the wop
Or the roto press that printed "Fiddle-dee-dee!"
In a three-color process all over Senator Sloop,
Just as he was making a speech. The thing about that
Was, how could it walk upstairs? But it was upstairs,
Clicking and mumbling in the Senate Chamber.
They had to knock out the wall to take it away
And the wrecking-crew said it grinned.

                             It was only the best
Machines, of course, the superhuman machines,
The ones we'd built to be better than flesh and bone,
But the cars were in it, of course . . .

                        and they hunted us
Like rabbits through the cramped streets on that Bloody
    Monday,
The Madison Avenue busses leading the charge.
The busses were pretty bad—but I'll not forget
The smash of glass when the Dusenberg left the show-room
And pinned three brokers to the Racquet Club steps
Or the long howl of the horns when they saw men run,
When they saw them looking for holes in the solid
    ground. . . .

I guess they were tired of being ridden in
And stopped and started by pygmies for silly ends,
Of wrapping cheap cigarettes and bad chocolate bars,
Collecting nickels and waving platinum hair
And letting six million people live in a town.
I guess it was that. I guess they got tired of us
And the whole smell of human hands.

                                                  But it was a shock
To climb sixteen flights of stairs to Art Zukow's office
(Nobody took the elevators twice)
And find him strangled to death in a nest of telephones,
The octopus-tendrils waving over his head,
And a sort of quiet humming filling the air. . . .
Do they eat? . . . There was red . . . But I did not stop
    to look.
I don't know yet how I got to a roof in time
And it's lonely, here on the roof.

                                       For a while, I thought
The window-cleaner would make it, and keep me company.
But they got him with his own hoist at the sixteenth floor
And dragged him in, with a squeal.
You see, they coöperate. Well, we taught them that
And it's fair enough, I suppose. You see, we built them.
We taught them to think for themselves.
It was bound to come. You can see it was bound to come.
And it won't be so bad, in the country. I hate to think
Of the reapers, running wild in the Kansas fields,
And the transport planes like hawks on a chickenyard,
But the horses might help. We might make a deal with the
    horses.
At least, you've more chance, out there.
                                  And they need us, too.

They're bound to realize that when they once calm down.
They'll need oil and spare parts and adjustments and tuning
        up.
Slaves? Well, in a way, you know, we were slaves before.
There won't be so much real difference—honest, there won't.
(I wish I hadn't looked into that beauty-parlor
And seen what was happening there.
But those are female machines and a bit high-strung.)
Oh, we'll settle down. We'll arrange it. We'll compromise.
It wouldn't make sense to wipe out the whole human race.
Why, I bet if I went to my old Plymouth now
(Of course you'd have to do it the tactful way)
And said, "Look here! Who got you the swell French
        horn?"
He wouldn't turn me over to those police cars;
At least I don't think he would.

                                    Oh, it's going to be jake.
There won't be so much real difference—honest, there
        won't—
And I'd go down in a minute and take my chance—
I'm a good American and I always liked them—
Except for one small detail that bothers me
And that's the food proposition. Because, you see,
The concrete-mixer may have made a mistake,
And it looks like just high spirits.
But, if it's got so they like the flavor . . . well . . .

Stephen Vincent Benét

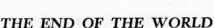

THE END OF THE WORLD

Quite unexpectedly as Vasserot
The armless ambidextrian was lighting
A match between his great and second toe
And Ralph the lion was engaged in biting
The neck of Madame Sossman while the drum
Pointed, and Teeny was about to cough
In waltz-time swinging Jocko by the thumb—
Quite unexpectedly the top blew off:

And there, there overhead, there, there, hung over
Those thousands of white faces, those dazed eyes,
There in the starless dark, the poise, the hover,
There with vast wings across the canceled skies,
There in the sudden blackness, the black pall
Of nothing, nothing, nothing—nothing at all.

Archibald MacLeish

THE BUSES HEADED FOR SCRANTON

The buses headed for Scranton travel in pairs.
The lead bus is the bolder,
With the taut appearance of one who greatly dares;
The driver glances constantly over his shoulder.

The buses headed for Scranton are sturdy craft,
Heavy-chested and chunky;
They have ample vision sideways and fore and aft;
The passengers brave, the pilots artful and spunky.

Children creep hand in hand up gloomy stairs;
The buses headed for Scranton travel in pairs.

They tell of a bus that headed for Scranton alone;
It dwindled into the West.
It was later found near a gasoline pump—moss-grown,
Deserted, abandoned, like the Mary Celeste.

Valises snuggled trimly upon the racks,
Lunches in tidy packets,
Twelve Daily Newses in neat, pathetic stacks,
Thermoses, Chiclets, and books with paper jackets.

Some say the travelers saw the Wendigo,
Or were eaten by bears.
I know not the horrid answer, I only know
That the buses headed for Scranton travel in pairs.

Ogden Nash

OVERHEARD ON A SALTMARSH

Nymph, nymph, what are your beads?

Green glass, goblin. Why do you stare at them?

Give them me.

      No.

Give them me. Give them me.

         No.

Then I will howl all night in the reeds,
Lie in the mud and howl for them.

Goblin, why do you love them so?

They are better than stars or water,
Better than voices of winds that sing,
Better than any man's fair daughter,
Your green glass beads on a silver ring.

Hush, I stole them out of the moon.

Give me your beads, I want them.

        No.

I will howl in a deep lagoon
For your green glass beads, I love them so.
Give them me. Give them.

No.

Harold Monro

THE WAY THROUGH THE WOODS

They shut the road through the woods
Seventy years ago.
Weather and rain have undone it again,
And now you would never know
There was once a road through the woods
Before they planted the trees.
It is underneath the coppice and heath
And the thin anemones.
Only the keeper sees
That, where the ring-dove broods,
And the badgers roll at ease,
There was once a road through the woods.

Yet, if you enter the woods
Of a summer evening late,
When the night-air cools on the trout-ringed pools
Where the otter whistles his mate,
(They fear not men in the woods,
Because they see so few.)
You will hear the beat of a horse's feet,
And the swish of a skirt in the dew,
Steadily cantering through
The misty solitudes,
As though they perfectly knew
The old lost road through the woods. . . .
But there is no road through the woods.

Rudyard Kipling

no time ago

no time ago
or else a life
walking in the dark
i met christ

jesus)my heart
flopped over
and lay still
while he passed(as

close as i'm to you
yes closer
made of nothing
except loneliness

E. E. Cummings

THE SONG OF THE WANDERING AENGUS

I went out to the hazel wood,
Because a fire was in my head,
And cut and peeled a hazel wand,
And hooked a berry to a thread.
And when white moths were on the wing,
And moth-like stars were flickering out,
I dropped the berry in a stream
And caught a little silver trout.

When I had laid it on the floor
I went to blow the fire a-flame,
But something rustled on the floor,
And someone called me by my name:
It had become a glimmering girl
With apple blossoms in her hair
Who called me by my name and ran
And faded through the brightening air.

Though I am old with wandering
Through hollow lands and hilly lands,
I will find out where she has gone,
And kiss her lips and take her hands;
And walk among long dappled grass,
And pluck till time and times are done,
The silver apples of the moon,
The golden apples of the sun.

William Butler Yeats

WITCHES' SONG

First Witch   Round about the cauldron go;
In the poison'd entrails throw.
Toad, that under cold stone
Days and nights has thirty-one
Swelter'd venom sleeping got,
Boil thou first i' the charmed pot.

All   Double, double toil and trouble;
Fire burn, and cauldron bubble.

Second Witch   Fillet of a fenny snake,
In the cauldron boil and bake;
Eye of newt and toe of frog,
Wool of bat and tongue of dog,
Adder's fork and blind-worm's sting,
Lizard's leg and howlet's wing,
For a charm of powerful trouble,
Like a hell-broth boil and bubble.

All   Double, double toil and trouble;
Fire burn, and cauldron bubble.

Third Witch   Scale of dragon, tooth of wolf,
Witches' mummy, maw and gulf
Of the ravin'd salt-sea shark,
Root of hemlock digged i' the dark

. . . .

Add thereto a tiger's chaudron,
For the ingredients of our cauldron.

All   Double, double toil and trouble;
Fire burn, and cauldron bubble.

William Shakespeare
MACBETH
ACT IV SCENE I

From "KUBLA KHAN"

Weave a circle round him thrice,
And close your eyes with holy dread,
For he on honey-dew hath fed,
And drunk the milk of Paradise.

Samuel Taylor Coleridge

THE BEES' SONG

Thouzandz of thornz there be
On the Rozez where gozez
The Zebra of Zee:
Sleek, striped, and hairy,
The steed of the Fairy
Princess of Zee.

Heavy with blozzomz be
The Rozez that growzez
In the thickets of Zee,
Where grazez the Zebra,
Marked Abracadeeebra
Of the Princess of Zee.

And he nozez the poziez
Of the Rozez that growzez
So luvez'm and free,
With an eye, dark and wary,
In search of a Fairy,
Whose Rozez he knowzez
Were not honeyed for he,
But to breathe a sweet incense
To solace the Princess
Of far-away Zee.

Walter de la Mare

DREAMS

Hold fast to dreams
For if dreams die
Life is a broken-winged bird
That cannot fly.

Hold fast to dreams
For when dreams go
Life is a barren field
Frozen with snow.

Langston Hughes

THE
ANIMAL
KINGDOM

THE BIRD

O clear and musical,
Sing again! Sing again!
Hear the rain fall
Through the long night.
Bring me your song again,
O dear delight!

O dear and comforting,
Mine again! Mine again!
Hear the rain sing
And dark rejoice!
Shine like a spark again,
O clearest voice!

Elinor Wylie

DOG AROUND THE BLOCK

Dog around the block, sniff,
Hydrant sniffing, corner, grating,
Sniffing, always, starting forward,
Backward, dragging, sniffing backward,
Leash at taut, leash at dangle,
Leash in people's feet entangle—
Sniffing dog, apprised of smellings,
Love of life, and fronts of dwellings,
Meeting enemies,
Loving old acquaintance, sniff,
Sniffing hydrant for reminders,
Leg against the wall, raise,
Leaving grating, corner greeting,
Chance for meeting, sniff, meeting,
Meeting, telling, news of smelling,
Nose to tail, tail to nose,
Rigid, careful, pose,
Liking, partly liking, hating,
Then another hydrant, grating,
Leash at taut, leash at dangle,
Tangle, sniff, untangle,
Dog around the block, sniff.

E. B. White

CAT'S FUNERAL

Bury her deep, down deep,
Safe in the earth's cold keep,
    Bury her deep—

No more to watch bird stir;
No more to clean dark fur;
No more to glisten as silk;
No more to revel in milk;
    No more to purr.

Bury her deep, down deep;
She is beyond warm sleep.
She will not walk in the night;
She will not wake to the light.
    Bury her deep.

E. V. Rieu

THE SNARE

I hear a sudden cry of pain!
    There is a rabbit in a snare:
Now I hear the cry again,
    But I cannot tell from where.

But I cannot tell from where
    He is calling out for aid!
Crying on the frightened air,
    Making everything afraid!

Making everything afraid!
    Wrinkling up his little face!
As he cries again for aid;
    —And I cannot find the place!

And I cannot find the place
    Where his paw is in the snare!
Little One! Oh, Little One!
    I am searching everywhere!

James Stephens

THE MEADOW MOUSE

In a shoe box stuffed in an old nylon stocking
Sleeps the baby mouse I found in the meadow,
Where he trembled and shook beneath a stick
Till I caught him up by the tail and brought him in,
Cradled in my hand,
A little quaker, the whole body of him trembling,
His absurd whiskers sticking out like a cartoon-mouse,
His feet like small leaves,
Little lizard feet,
Whitish and spread wide when he tried to struggle away,
Wiggling like a miniscule puppy.

Now he's eaten his three kinds of cheese and drunk from
       his bottle-cap watering-trough—
So much he just lies in one corner,
His tail curled under him, his belly big
As his head; his bat-like ears
Twitching, tilting toward the least sound.
Do I imagine he no longer trembles
When I come close to him?
He seems no longer to tremble.

II

But this morning the shoe-box house on the back porch is
       empty.
Where has he gone, my meadow mouse,
My thumb of a child that nuzzled in my palm?—

45

To run under the hawk's wing,
Under the eye of the great owl watching from the elm-tree,
To live by courtesy of the shrike, the snake, the tom-cat.

I think of the nestling fallen into the deep grass,
The turtle gasping in the dusty rubble of the highway,
The paralytic stunned in the tub, and the water rising,—
All things innocent, hapless, forsaken.

Theodore Roethke

THE SEAL'S LULLABY

Oh! hush thee, my baby, the night is behind us,
    And black are the waters that sparkled so green.
The moon, o'er the combers, looks downwards to find us
    At rest in the hollows that rustle between.
Where billow meets billow, then soft be thy pillow,
    Oh, weary wee flipperling curl at thy ease!
The storm shall not wake thee, nor shark overtake thee,
    Asleep in the arms of the slow-swinging seas!

Rudyard Kipling

DEPARTMENTAL

An ant on the table cloth
Ran into a dormant moth
Of many times his size.
He showed not the least surprise.
His business wasn't with such.
He gave it scarcely a touch,
And was off on his duty run.
Yet if he encountered one
Of the hive's enquiry squad
Whose work is to find out God
And the nature of time and space,
He would put him onto the case.
Ants are a curious race;
One crossing with hurried tread
The body of one of their dead
Isn't given a moment's arrest—
Seems not even impressed.
But he no doubt reports to any
With whom he crosses antennae,
And they no doubt report
To the higher up at court.
Then word goes forth in Formic:
'Death's come to Jerry McCormic,
Our selfless forager Jerry.
Will the special Janizary
Whose office it is to bury
The dead of the commissary

Go bring him home to his people.
Lay him in state on a sepal.
Wrap him for shroud in a petal.
Embalm him with ichor of nettle.
This is the word of your Queen.'
And presently on the scene
Appears a solemn mortician;
And taking formal position
With feelers calmly atwiddle,
Seizes the dead by the middle,
And heaving him high in air,
Carries him out of there.
No one stands round to stare.
It is nobody else's affair.

It couldn't be called ungentle.
But how thoroughly departmental.

Robert Frost

THE BAT BABY

A bat is born
Naked and blind and pale.
His mother makes a pocket of her tail
And catches him. He clings to her long fur
By his thumbs and toes and teeth.
And then the mother dances through the night
Doubling and looping, soaring, somersaulting—
Her baby hangs on underneath.
All night in happiness she hunts and flies.

Randall Jarrell

THE PRAYER OF THE OX

Dear God, give me time.
    Men are always so driven!
    Make them understand that I can never hurry.
    Give me time to eat.
    Give me time to plod.
    Give me time to sleep.
    Give me time to think.

Amen

TRANSLATED BY
Rumer Godden

SNAIL

Little snail,
Dreaming you go.
Weather and rose
Is all you know.

Weather and rose
Is all you see,
Drinking
The dewdrop's
Mystery.

Langston Hughes

LOVE
AND
KISSES

OH, WHEN I WAS IN LOVE

Oh, when I was in love with you,
    Then I was clean and brave,
And miles around the wonder grew
    How well did I behave.

And now the fancy passes by,
    And nothing will remain,
And miles around they'll say that I
    Am quite myself again.

A. E. Housman

LOVE POEM

My clumsiest dear, whose hands shipwreck vases,
At whose quick touch all glasses chip and ring,
Whose palms are bulls in china, burs in linen,
And have no cunning with any soft thing

Except all ill-at-ease fidgeting people:
The refugee uncertain at the door
You make at home; deftly you steady
The drunk clambering on his undulant floor.

Unpredictable dear, the taxi drivers' terror,
Shrinking from far headlights pale as a dime
Yet leaping before red apoplectic streetcars—
Misfit in any space. And never on time.

A wrench in clocks and the solar system. Only
With words and people and love you move at ease.
In traffic of wit expertly manoeuvre
And keep us, all devotion, at your knees.

Forgetting your coffee spreading on our flannel,
Your lipstick grinning on our coat,
So gayly in love's unbreakable heaven
Our souls on glory of spilt bourbon float.

Be with me darling, early and late. Smash glasses—
I will study wry music for your sake.
For should your hands drop white and empty
All the toys of the world would break.

John Frederick Nims

A SUBALTERN'S LOVE-SONG

Miss J. Hunter Dunn, Miss J. Hunter Dunn,
Furnish'd and burnish'd by Aldershot sun,
What strenuous singles we played after tea,
We in the tournament—you against me!

Love-thirty, love-forty, oh! weakness of joy,
The speed of a swallow, the grace of a boy,
With carefullest carelessness, gaily you won,
I am weak from your loveliness, Joan Hunter Dunn.

Miss Joan Hunter Dunn, Miss Joan Hunter Dunn,
How mad I am, sad I am, glad that you won.
The warm-handled racket is back in its press,
But my shock-headed victor, she loves me no less.

Her father's euonymus shines as we walk,
And swing past the summer-house, buried in talk,
And cool the verandah that welcomes us in
To the six-o'clock news and a lime-juice and gin.

The scent of the conifers, sound of the bath,
The view from my bedroom of moss-dappled path,
As I struggle with double-end evening tie.
For we dance at the Golf Club, my victor and I.

On the floor of her bedroom lie blazer and shorts
And the cream-coloured walls are be-trophied with sports,
And westering, questioning settles the sun
On your low-leaded window, Miss Joan Hunter Dunn.

The Hillman is waiting, the light's in the hall,
The pictures of Egypt are bright on the wall,
My sweet, I am standing beside the oak stair
And there on the landing's the light on your hair.

By roads "not adopted," by woodlanded ways,
She drove to the club in the late summer haze,
Into nine-o'clock Camberley, heavy with bells
And mushroomy, pine-woody, evergreen smells.

Miss Joan Hunter Dunn, Miss Joan Hunter Dunn,
I can hear from the car-park the dance has begun.
Oh! full Surrey twilight! importunate band!
Oh! strongly adorable tennis-girl's hand!

Around us are Rovers and Austins afar,
Above us, the intimate roof of the car,
And here on my right is the girl of my choice,
With the tilt of her nose and the chime of her voice,

And the scent of her wrap, and the words never said,
And the ominous, ominous dancing ahead.
We sat in the car-park till twenty to one
And now I'm engaged to Miss Joan Hunter Dunn.

John Betjeman

❀

DIALOGUE

Jaques—Rosalind is your love's name?

Orlando—Yes, just.

Jaques—I do not like her name.

Orlando—There was no thought of pleasing you
   when she was christened.

Jaques—What stature is she of?

Orlando—Just as high as my heart.

William Shakespeare
AS YOU LIKE IT
ACT III SCENE II

THE PASSIONATE SHEPHERD TO HIS LOVE

Come live with me and be my Love,
And we will all the pleasures prove
That hills and valleys, dales and fields,
Or woods or steepy mountain yields.

And we will sit upon the rocks,
And see the shepherds feed their flocks
By shallow rivers, to whose falls
Melodious birds sing madrigals.

And I will make thee beds of roses
And a thousand fragrant posies;
A cap of flowers, and a kirtle
Embroidered all with leaves of myrtle.

A gown made of the finest wool
Which from our pretty lambs we pull;
Fair-lined slippers for the cold,
With buckles of the purest gold.

A belt of straw and ivy-buds
With coral clasps and amber studs;
And if these pleasures may thee move,
Come live with me and be my Love.

Christopher Marlowe

LOVE UNDER THE REPUBLICANS
(OR DEMOCRATS)

Come live with me and be my love
And we will all the pleasures prove
Of a marriage conducted with economy
In the Twentieth Century Anno Donomy.
We'll live in a dear little walk-up flat
With practically room to swing a cat
And a potted cactus to give it hauteur
And a bathtub equipped with dark brown water.
We'll eat, without undue discouragement
Foods low in cost but high in nouragement
And quaff with pleasure, while chatting wittily,
The peculiar wine of Little Italy.
We'll remind each other it's smart to be thrifty
And buy our clothes for something-fifty.
We'll stand in line on holidays
For seats at unpopular matinees,
And every Sunday we'll have a lark
And take a walk in Central Park.
And one of these days not too remote
I'll probably up and cut your throat.

Ogden Nash

FOR ANNE GREGORY

'Never shall a young man,
Thrown into despair
By those great honey-coloured
Ramparts at your ear,
Love you for yourself alone
And not your yellow hair.'

'But I can get a hair-dye
And set such colour there,
Brown, or black, or carrot,
That young men in despair
May love me for myself alone
And not my yellow hair.'

'I heard an old religious man
But yesternight declare
That he had found a text to prove
That only God, my dear,
Could love you for yourself alone
And not your yellow hair.'

William Butler Yeats

WHEN TROUT SWIM DOWN
GREAT ORMOND STREET

When trout swim down Great Ormond Street,
And sea-gulls cry above them lightly,
And hawthorns heave cold flagstones up
To blossom whitely,

Against old walls of houses there,
Gustily shaking out in moonlight
Their country sweetness on sweet air;
And in the sunlight,

By the green margin of that water,
Children dip white feet and shout,
Casting nets in the braided water
To catch the trout:

Then I shall hold my breath and die,
Swearing I never loved you; no,
'You were not lovely!' I shall cry,
'I never loved you so.'

Conrad Aiken

AN IMMORALITY

Sing we for love and idleness,
Naught else is worth the having.

Though I have been in many a land,
There is naught else in living.

And I would rather have my sweet,
Though rose-leaves die of grieving,

Than do high deeds in Hungary
To pass all men's believing.

Ezra Pound

UPON HIS MISTRESS DANCING

I stood and saw my mistress dance,
    Silent, and with so fixed an eye,
Some might suppose me in a trance.
    But being askëd, why?
By one that knew I was in love,
    I could not but impart
My wonder, to behold her move
    So nimbly with a marble heart.

James Shirley

LOVE SONG

My own dear love, he is strong and bold
    And he cares not what comes after.
His words ring sweet as a chime of gold,
    And his eyes are lit with laughter.
He is jubilant as a flag unfurled—
    Oh, a girl, she'd not forget him.
My own dear love, he is all my world—
    And I wish I'd never met him.

My love, he's mad, and my love, he's fleet,
    And a wild young wood-thing bore him!
The ways are fair to his roaming feet,
    And the skies are sunlit for him.
As sharply sweet to my heart he seems
    As the fragrance of acacia.
My own dear love, he is all my dreams—
    And I wish he were in Asia.

My love runs by like a day in June,
    And he makes no friends of sorrows.
He'll tread his galloping rigadoon
    In the pathway of the morrows.
He'll live his days where the sunbeams start,
    Nor could storm or wind uproot him.
My own dear love, he is all my heart—
    And I wish somebody'd shoot him.

Dorothy Parker

GENTLEMEN
AND
LADIES

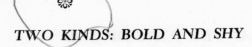

TWO KINDS: BOLD AND SHY

Shy thinks, "They are all looking at me now.
I hope my necktie is not skewed about.
I must keep quiet here, no matter how.
My voice might squeak, or fail me. I might shout
For very shyness. That girl laughed at me.
I knew my clothes and face and name were wrong.
Let me alone. Ignore me utterly.
How long will this party last, O Lord, how long?"

Bold says, and says it boldly, "I am here.
Everyone knows me well, saw me come in.
Now I am speaking. Lend a willing ear.
This is the way your party should begin.
You like me. I am liked as much as any,
And I say I deserve it more than many."

John Holmes

I MARVEL AT THE WAYS OF GOD

I marvel at the ways of God,
    For time and time again
I see Him paint such lovely clouds
    Above such awkward men.

E. B. White

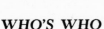

WHO'S WHO

A shilling life will give you all the facts:
How Father beat him, how he ran away,
What were the struggles of his youth, what acts
Made him the greatest figure of his day:
Of how he fought, fished, hunted, worked all night;
Though giddy, climbed new mountains; named a sea:
Some of the last researchers even write
Love made him weep his pints like you and me.

With all his honours on, he sighed for one
Who, say astonished critics, lived at home;
Did little jobs about the house with skill
And nothing else; could whistle; would sit still
Or potter round the garden; answered some
Of his long marvellous letters but kept none.

W. H. Auden

EPITAPH FOR A GRIM WOMAN

Sharp as sword of Saracen,
    Her fierce, New England pride:
She whetted it for years, and then
    She fell on it and died!

Patience Eden

BLUE GIRLS

Twirling your blue skirts, travelling the sward
Under the towers of your seminary,
Go listen to your teachers old and contrary
Without believing a word.

Tie the white fillets then about your lustrous hair
And think no more of what will come to pass
Than bluebirds that go walking on the grass
And chattering on the air.

Practice your beauty, blue girls, before it fail;
And I will cry with my loud lips and publish
Beauty which all our power shall never establish,
It is so frail.

For I could tell you a story which is true:
I know a lady with a terrible tongue,
Blear eyes fallen from blue,
All her perfections tarnished—yet it is not long
Since she was lovelier than any of you.

John Crowe Ransom

IN SCHRAFFT'S

Having finished the Blue-plate Special
And reached the coffee stage,
Stirring her cup she sat,
A somewhat shapeless figure
Of indeterminate age
In an undistinguished hat.

When she lifted her eyes it was plain
That our globular furore,
Our international rout
Of sin and apparatus
And dying men galore,
Was not being bothered about.

Which of the seven heavens
Was responsible her smile
Wouldn't be sure but attested
That, whoever it was, a god
Worth kneeling-to for a while
Had tabernacled and rested.

W. H. Auden

SILENCE

My father used to say,
"Superior people never make long visits,"
have to be shown Longfellow's grave
or the glass flowers at Harvard.
Self-reliant like the cat—
that takes its prey to privacy,
the mouse's limp tail hanging like a shoelace from its mouth—
they sometimes enjoy solitude,
and can be robbed of speech
by speech which has delighted them.
The deepest feeling always shows itself in silence;
not in silence, but restraint.
Nor was he insincere in saying, "Make my house your inn."
Inns are not residences.

Marianne Moore

OLD MEN AND YOUNG MEN

Old men are full of zest and information,
And they remember all they ever thought.
Old men are vigorous in conversation.
Young men exist to listen and be taught.
Old men give dates that may not be disputed,
And they remember parts old actors played.
A young man's fact is easily refuted:
He was not present when the world was made.

Old men are heartily opinionated.
Whatever young men do, the old have done
In better ways that have not deviated.
The legend lies, that old men sit in the sun.
Old men, in great ambition unabated,
Stand proudly on their heads at eighty-one.

Young men are thin and shy, which is no wonder:
Young men need rest, and life allows them none.
The old men storm at them for every blunder.
Nothing is right young men have ever done.
Young men who tell a story twitch and stutter.
Their ears are large and red. Their hands are cold.
They speak too loud, or in despair they mutter,
And feel discouraged when the story's told.

Old men resent solicitude and hearses.
All they abstained from doing they regret.

Old men betrayed into the hands of nurses
Despise the scientific care they get,
And vow disgracefully, with terrible curses,
That they'll outlive the meddling woman yet.

John Holmes

"THIS QUIET DUST . . ."

This quiet dust was Gentlemen and Ladies,
    And Lads and Girls;
Was laughter and ability and sighing,
    And frocks and curls.
This passive place a Summer's nimble mansion,
    Where Bloom and Bees
Fulfilled their Oriental Circuit,
    Then ceased like these.

Emily Dickinson

THE
POISON
PEN

A GLASS OF BEER

The lanky hank of a she in the inn over there
Nearly killed me for asking the loan of a glass of beer;
May the devil grip the whey-faced slut by the hair,
And beat bad manners out of her skin for a year.

That parboiled ape, with the toughest jaw you will see
On virtue's path, and a voice that would rasp the dead,
Came roaring and raging the minute she looked at me,
And threw me out of the house on the back of my head!

If I asked her master he'd give me a cask a day;
But she, with the beer at hand, not a gill would arrange!
May she marry a ghost and bear him a kitten, and may
The High King of Glory permit her to get the mange.

FROM THE IRISH BY
James Stephens

GEORGE III

George the Third
Ought never to have occurred.
One can only wonder
At so grotesque a blunder.

Edmund Clerihew Bentley

ELEGY IN A COUNTRY CHURCHYARD

The men that worked for England
They have their graves at home:
And bees and birds of England
About the cross can roam.

But they that fought for England,
Following a falling star,
Alas, alas for England
They have their graves afar.

And they that rule in England,
In stately conclave met,
Alas, alas for England
They have no graves as yet.

G. K. Chesterton

BRUADAR AND SMITH AND GLINN

Bruadar and Smith and Glinn,
　　Amen, dear God, I pray
May they lie low in waves of woe,
　　And tortures slow each day.
　　　　　　　　　Amen!

Blindness come down on Smith,
　　Palsy on Bruadar come,
Amen, O King of Brightness! Smite
　　Glinn in his members numb.
　　　　　　　　　Amen!

For Bruadar gape the grave,
　　Up-shovel for Smith the mould,
Amen, O King of the Sunday! Leave
　　Glinn in the devil's hold.
　　　　　　　　　Amen!

Hell-hounds to hunt for Smith,
　　Glinn to hang on high,
Amen, O King of the Judgment Day!
　　And Bruadar rotting by.
　　　　　　　　　Amen!

Each of the wicked three
　　Who raised against me their hand,
May fire from heaven come down and slay
　　This day their perjured band.
　　　　　　　　　Amen!

May none of their race survive,
    May God destroy them all,
Each curse of the psalms in the holy books
    Of the prophets upon them fall.
                    Amen!

Blight skull, and ear, and skin,
    And hearing, and voice, and sight,
Amen! before the year be out
    Blight, Son of the Virgin, blight.
                    Amen!

FROM THE IRISH BY
Douglas Hyde

THE HUMAN RACE

I wish I loved the Human Race;
I wish I loved its silly face;
I wish I liked the way it walks;
I wish I liked the way it talks;
And when I'm introduced to one
I wish I thought What Jolly Fun!

Sir Walter Raleigh

ON CHARLES II

Here lies our sovereign lord the king,
    Whose word no man relies on:
He never says a foolish thing,
    Nor ever does a wise one.*

Lord Rochester (1647–1680)

* To which epigram Charles II replied: "My sayings are my own, my actions are my ministers'."

CORIOLANUS'S FAREWELL TO HIS FELLOW-CITIZENS AS HE GOES INTO BANISHMENT

You common cry of curs! whose breath I hate
As reek o' the rotten fens, whose loves I prize
As the dead carcasses of unburied men
That do corrupt my air, I banish you;
And here remain with your uncertainty!
Let every feeble rumour shake your hearts!
Your enemies, with nodding of their plumes,
Fan you into despair; have the power still
To banish your defenders; till at length
Your ignorance—which finds not, till it feels—
Making not reservation of yourselves,—
Still your own foes,—deliver you as most
Abated captives to some nation
That won you without blows!

William Shakespeare
CORIOLANUS
ACT III SCENE III

ON A POLITICIAN

Here, richly, with ridiculous display,
The Politician's corpse was laid away.
While all of his acquaintance sneered and slanged,
I wept; for I had longed to see him hanged.

Hilaire Belloc

I WISH MY TONGUE WERE A QUIVER

I wish my tongue were a quiver the size of a huge cask
Packed and crammed with long black venomous
    rankling darts.
I'd fling you more full of them, and joy in the task,
Than ever Sebastian was, or Caesar, with thirty-three
    swords in his heart.

I'd make a porcupine out of you, or a pin-cushion, say:
The shafts should stand so thick you'd look like a
    headless hen
Hung up by the heels, with the long bare red neck
    stretching, curving, and dripping away
From the soiled floppy ball of ruffled feathers standing
    on end.

You should bristle like those cylindrical brushes they
    use to scrub out bottles,
Not even to reach the kindly earth with the soles of
    your prickled feet.
And I would stand by and watch you wriggle and
    writhe, gurgling through the barbs in your throttle
Like a woolly caterpillar pinned on its back—man, that
    would be sweet.

L. A. Mackay

TIT FOR TAT

My slayer buried me to ease his mind.
God send his kindness be repaid in kind.

Anonymous

TRUMPET
SOUNDS

FIFE TUNE

6/8 for Sixth Platoon, 308th I.T.C.

One morning in spring
We marched from Devizes
All shapes and all sizes
Like beads on a string,
But yet with a swing
We trod the blue metal
And full of high fettle
We started to sing.

She ran down the stair
A twelve-year-old darling
And laughing and calling
She tossed her bright hair;
Then silent to stare
At the men flowing past her—
There were all she could master
Adoring her there.

It's seldom I'll see
A sweeter or prettier;
I doubt we'll forget her
In two years or three,
And lucky he'll be
She takes for a lover
While we are far over
The treacherous sea.

John Manifold

OH STAY AT HOME

Oh stay at home, my lad, and plough
    The land and not the sea,
And leave the soldiers at their drill,
And all about the idle hill
    Shepherd your sheep with me.

Oh stay with company and mirth
    And daylight and the air;
Too full already is the grave
Of fellows that were good and brave
    And died because they were.

A. E. Housman

THE GENERAL

"Good-morning; good-morning!" the General said
When we met him last week on our way to the line.
Now the soldiers he smiled at are most of 'em dead,
And we're cursing his staff for incompetent swine.
"He's a cheery old card," grunted Harry to Jack
As they slogged up to Arras with rifle and pack.

.   .   .   .

But he did for them both by his plan of attack.

Siegfried Sassoon

✿

HENRY'S ADDRESS TO HIS TROOPS

This day is called the Feast of Crispian.
He that outlives this day, and comes safe home,
Will stand a-tiptoe when this day is named
And rouse him at the name of Crispian.

He that shall live this day, and see old age,
Will yearly on the vigil feast his neighbors
And say, 'To-morrow is Saint Crispian.'
Then will he strip his sleeve and show his scars,
And say, 'These wounds I had on Crispin's day.'

Old men forget; yet all shall be forgot,
But he'll remember, with advantages,
What feats he did that day. Then shall our names,
Familiar in his mouth as household words—
Harry the King, Bedford and Exeter,
Warwick and Talbot, Salisbury and Gloucester—
Be in their flowing cups freshly rememb'red.

This story shall the good man teach his son;
And Crispin Crispian shall ne'er go by,
From this day to the ending of the world,
But we in it shall be remembered—
We few, we happy few, we band of brothers;

For he to-day that sheds his blood with me
Shall be my brother; be he ne'er so vile,
This day shall gentle his condition;

And gentlemen in England now abed
Shall think themselves accursed they were not here,
And hold their manhoods cheap whiles any speaks
That fought with us upon Saint Crispin's day.

William Shakespeare
KING HENRY V
ACT IV SCENE III

❧

THE HAND THAT SIGNED THE PAPER

The hand that signed the paper felled a city;
Five sovereign fingers taxed the breath,
Doubled the globe of dead and halved a country;
These five kings did a king to death.

The mighty hand leads to a sloping shoulder,
The finger joints are cramped with chalk;
A goose's quill has put an end to murder
That put an end to talk.

The hand that signed the treaty bred a fever,
And famine grew, and locusts came;
Great is the hand that holds dominion over
Man by a scribbled name.

The five kings count the dead but do not soften
The crusted wound nor pat the brow;
A hand rules pity as a hand rules heaven;
Hands have no tears to flow.

Dylan Thomas

TO LUCASTA, ON GOING TO THE WARS

Tell me not, Sweet, I am unkind
 That from the nunnery
Of thy chaste breast, and quiet mind,
 To war and arms I fly.

True, a new mistress now I chase,
 The first foe in the field;
And with a stronger faith embrace
 A sword, a horse, a shield.

Yet this inconstancy is such
 As you too shall adore;
I could not love thee, Dear, so much,
 Loved I not honor more.

Richard Lovelace

THE CRIMEAN WAR HEROES

Hail, ye indomitable heroes, hail!
Despite of all your generals ye prevail.

Walter Savage Landor

THE WAR SONG OF DINAS VAWR

The mountain sheep are sweeter,
But the valley sheep are fatter;
We therefore deemed it meeter
To carry off the latter.
We made an expedition;
We met a host and quelled it;
We forced a strong position,
And killed the men who held it.

On Dyfed's richest valley,
Where herds of kine were browsing,
We made a mighty sally,
To furnish our carousing.
Fierce warriors rushed to meet us;
We met them, and o'erthrew them:
They struggled hard to beat us;
But we conquered them, and slew them.

As we drove our prize at leisure,
The king marched forth to catch us:
His rage surpassed all measure,
But his people could not match us.
He fled to his hall-pillars;
And, ere our force we led off,
Some sacked his house and cellars,
While others cut his head off.

We there, in strife bewildering,
Spilt blood enough to swim in:
We orphaned many children,
And widowed many women.
The eagles and the ravens
We glutted with our foemen:
The heroes and the cravens,
The spearmen and the bowmen.

We brought away from battle,
And much their land bemoaned them,
Two thousand head of cattle,
And the head of him who owned them:
Ednyfed, King of Dyfed,
His head was borne before us;
His wine and beasts supplied our feasts,
And his overthrow, our chorus.

Thomas Love Peacock

1936

All night they marched, the infantrymen under pack,
But the hands gripping the rifles were naked bone
And the hollow pits of the eyes stared, vacant and black,
When the moonlight shone.

The gas mask lay like a blot on the empty chest,
The slanting helmets were spattered with rust and mold,
But they borrowed the hill for the machine-gun nest
As they had of old.

And the guns rolled, and the tanks, but there was no sound,
Never the gasp or rustle of living men
Where the skeletons strung their wire on disputed
    ground . . . .
I knew them, then.

"It is eighteen years," I cried. "You must come no more."
"We know your names. We know that you are the dead.
Must you march forever from France and the last, blind
    war?"
"*Fool! From the next!*" they said.

                                    Stephen Vincent Benét

FAR-OFF
PLACES

THE CLOSING OF THE RODEO

The lariat snaps; the cowboy rolls
    His pack, and mounts and rides away.
Back to the land the cowboy goes.

Plumes of smoke from the factory sway
    In the setting sun. The curtain falls,
A train in the darkness pulls away.

Good-by, says the rain on the iron roofs.
    Good-by, say the barber poles.
Dark drum the vanishing horses' hooves.

William Jay Smith

ITALIAN EXCURSION

In Cecina the solacing words were over a portal:
"This is the house of God and the door of heaven."

In Padua there was a soldier shaving,
At home in the quiet cloisters of the cathedral.

In Venice a man was singing "O Paradiso,"
Not in a gondola, on a morning ferry.

In a café at Verona they had a painting
Of Christ and the Sacred Heart over the bar.

In Milan across the square from the silver cathedral
Glittered the sign *Bevete Coca-Cola*.

Helen Bevington

ROMANCE

When I was but thirteen or so
    I went into a golden land,
Chimborazo, Cotopaxi
    Took me by the hand.

My father died, my brother too,
    They passed like fleeting dreams.
I stood where Popocatapetl
    In the sunlight gleams.

I dimly heard the Master's voice
    And boys far-off at play,
Chimborazo, Cotopaxi
    Had stolen me away.

I walked in a great golden dream
    To and fro from school—
Shining Popocatapetl
    The dusty streets did rule.

I walked home with a gold dark boy
    And never a word I'd say,
Chimborazo, Cotopaxi
    Had taken my speech away:

I gazed entranced upon his face
    Fairer than any flower—
O shining Popocatapetl
    It was thy magic hour:

The houses, people, traffic seemed
    Thin fading dreams by day,
Chimborazo, Cotopaxi
    They had stolen my soul away!

Walter J. Turner

AT THE AIRPORT

Through the gate, where nowhere and night begin,
A hundred suddenly appear and lose
Themselves in the hot and crowded waiting room.
A hundred other herd up toward the gate,
Patiently waiting that the way be opened
To nowhere and night, while a voice recites
The intermittent litany of numbers
And the holy names of distant destinations.

None going out can be certain of getting there.
None getting there can be certain of being loved
Enough. But they are sealed in the silver tube
And lifted up to be fed and cosseted,
While their upholstered cell of warmth and light
Shatters the darkness, neither here nor there.

Howard Nemerov

LETTER TO N.Y.

In your next letter I wish you'd say
where you are going and what you are doing;
how are the plays, and after the plays
what other pleasures you're pursuing:

taking cabs in the middle of the night,
driving as if to save your soul
where the road goes round and round the park
and the meter glares like a moral owl,

and the trees look so queer and green
standing alone in big black caves
and suddenly you're in a different place
where everything seems to happen in waves,

and most of the jokes you just can't catch,
like dirty words rubbed off a slate,
and the songs are loud but somehow dim
and it gets so terribly late,

and coming out of the brownstone house
to the gray sidewalk, the watered street,
one side of the buildings rises with the sun
like a glistening field of wheat.

—Wheat, not oats, dear. I'm afraid
if it's wheat it's none of your sowing,
nevertheless I'd like to know
what you are doing and where you are going.

Elizabeth Bishop

I MAY, I MIGHT, I MUST

If you will tell me why the fen
appears impassable, I then
will tell you why I think that I
can get across it if I try.

Marianne Moore

CROSSING KANSAS BY TRAIN

The telephone poles
have been holding their
arms out
a long time now
to birds
that will not
settle there
but pass with
strange cawings
westward to
where dark trees
gather about
a waterhole. This
is Kansas. The
mountains start here
just behind
the closed eyes
of a farmer's
sons asleep
in their workclothes.

Donald Justice

THE COLORADO TRAIL

Eyes like the morning star,
    Cheek like a rose,
Laura was a pretty girl,
    God Almighty knows.

Weep, all ye little rains,
    Wail, winds, wail,
All along, along, along
    The Colorado trail.

American Folk Song

THE
CHANGING
YEAR

SUNDAY

The gentlemen's sticks swing extra high,
So sharp the air, so March the sky;
The gentlemen's steps are extra spry
And gentlemen's hats are silk and high,
    When Millicent takes me walking.

The lady-fairs' boots are zippered tight,
So bleak the wind, so near the night;
And lady-fairs' noses are red, not white;
It's hardly an advantageous light
    When Millicent takes me walking.

The little dogs' robes are buckled fast,
So chill the day, so swift the blast;
On three-skip-one they patter past,
Oh, little dogs' legs go extra fast
    When Millicent takes me walking!

The icicles cling to the funniest things,
To a red moustache, to a griffin's wings,
To the under side of a Buick's springs,
Oh, an icicle doesn't care where it clings
    When Millicent takes me walking!

Oh, gentlemen's sticks swing extra high,
And sharp the air and March the sky,
And lady-fairs' boots are zippered tight,
Oh, bleak the wind, oh, near the night!

And little dogs' robes are buckled fast,
So chill the day, so swift the blast,
And icicles don't care where they cling—
Yet Millicent says it will soon be Spring
When Millicent takes me walking!

E. B. White

VERNAL SENTIMENT

Though the crocuses poke up their heads in the usual places,
The frog scum appear on the pond with the same froth of
    green,
And boys moon at girls with last year's fatuous faces,
I never am bored, however familiar the scene.

When from under the barn the cat brings a similar litter,—
Two yellow and black, and one that looks in between,—
Though it all happened before, I cannot grow bitter:
I rejoice in the spring, as though no spring ever had been.

Theodore Roethke

SPRING

Now rouses Earth, so long quiescent,
    To kiss and curse her fate,
In storm of bliss or woe incessant,
    Despairing or elate.
She's only being adolescent;
    Nothing to do but wait.

Morris Bishop

SONG

the
    sky
        was
can dy lu
minous
        edible
spry
    pinks shy
lemons
greens coo l choc
olate
s.

  un der,
 a lo
co
mo
    tive s pout
            ing
          vi
          o
          lets

E. E. Cummings

RONDEAU

The world is taking off her clothes
Of snowdrift, rain and strait-laced freeze
And turns, to show forth by degrees
The bosom of a Rose La Rose.

There's not a bud nor bird, Lord knows,
Can keep still in its balconies.
The world is taking off her clothes
Of snowdrift, rain and strait-laced freeze.

Brook become great from melted snows
Wears a last stitch of ice to tease
And sequined, river's last chemise
Undone in a shudder goes—
The world is taking off her clothes.

X. J. Kennedy

THE WAKING

I strolled across
An open field;
The sun was out;
Heat was happy.

This way! This way!
The wren's throat shimmered,
Either to other,
The blossoms sang.

The stones sang,
The little ones did,
And flowers jumped
Like small goats.

A ragged fringe
Of daisies waved;
I wasn't alone
In a grove of apples.

Far in the wood
A nestling sighed;
The dew loosened
Its morning smells.

I came where the river
Ran over stones:

My ears knew
An early joy.

And all the waters
Of all the streams
Sang in my veins
That summer day.

Theodore Roethke

NO!

No sun—no moon!
No morn—no noon—
No dawn—no dusk—no proper time of day—
No sky—no earthly view—
No distance looking blue—
No road—no street—no "t'other side the way"—
No end to any Row—
No indications where the Crescents go—
No top to any steeple—
No recognitions of familiar people—
No courtesies for showing 'em—
No knowing 'em!—
No travelling at all—no locomotion,
No inkling of the way—no notion—
"No go"—by land or ocean—
No mail—no post—
No news from any foreign coast—
No Park—no Ring—no afternoon gentility—
No company—no nobility—
No warmth, no cheerfulness, no healthful ease,
No comfortable feel in any member—
No shade, no shine, no butterflies, no bees,
No fruits, no flowers, no leaves, no birds,—
November!

Thomas Hood

SONG FOR SNOW

The earth is lighter
Than the sky,
The world is wider
Than in spring.
Along white roads
The sleighs go by,
Icily sweet
The sleighbells ring.

The birds are gone
Into the South,
The leaves are fallen
To the ground,
But singing shakes
Each sleighbell's mouth
And leaf-like ears
Turn to the sound.

Elizabeth Coatsworth

✿

WHEN COLD DECEMBER

When cold December
Froze to grisamber
The jangling bells on the sweet rose-trees—
Then fading slow
And furred is the snow
As the almond's sweet husk—
And smelling like musk.
The snow amygdaline
Under the eglantine
Where bristling stars shine
Like a gilt porcupine—
The snow confesses
The little Princesses
On their small chioppines
Dance under the orpines.
See the casuistries
Of their slant fluttering eyes—
Gilt as the zodiac
(Dancing Herodiac).
Only the snow slides
Like gilded myrrh—
From the rose-branches—hides
Rose-roots that stir.

Edith Sitwell

RELATIVELY
SPEAKING

TO MY SON

Go, and be gay;
You are born into the dazzling light of day.
Go, and be wise;
You are born upon an earth which needs new eyes.
Go, and be strong;
You are born into a world where love rights wrong.
Go, and be brave;
Possess your soul; that you alone can save.

Siegfried Sassoon

SHORT HISTORY OF MAN

Quick! Grab the baby, the precious pet.
He'll pitch right out of his bassinet.
Hey! Raise the side of the fellow's crib.
He's getting over. He'll crack a rib.
Look out! Today is the day he dares
Climb the gate at the top of the stairs.
Go get him! He's out in the entrance-hall.
I thought his play-pen looked too small.
Hurry up there! Fence the garden in
As high as a very tall man's chin.
Come on! He's learned to lift the latch,
And I have an idea he's hard to catch.
Run! Run faster! We're still too slow.
What do you say if we let him go?

John Holmes

nobody loses all the time

i had an uncle named
Sol who was a born failure and
nearly everybody said he should have gone
into vaudeville perhaps because my Uncle Sol could
sing McCann He was A Diver on Xmas Eve like Hell Itself which
may or may not account for the fact that my Uncle

Sol indulged in that possibly most inexcusable
of all to use a highfalootin phrase
luxuries that is or to
wit farming and be
it needlessly
added

my Uncle Sol's farm
failed because the chickens
ate the vegetables so
my Uncle Sol had a
chicken farm till the
skunks ate the chickens when

my Uncle Sol
had a skunk farm but
the skunks caught cold and
died and so
my Uncle Sol imitated the
skunks in a subtle manner

or by drowning himself in the watertank
but somebody who'd given my Uncle Sol a Victor
Victrola and records while he lived presented to
him upon the auspicious occasion of his decease a
scrumptious not to mention splendiferous funeral with
tall boys in black gloves and flowers and everything and

i remember we all cried like the Missouri
when my Uncle Sol's coffin lurched because
somebody pressed a button
(and down went
my Uncle
Sol

and started a worm farm)

                                              E. E. Cummings

A FATHER SWINGS HIS CHILD

Here in the scuffled dust
    is our ground of play.
I lift you on your swing and must
    shove you away,
see you return again,
    drive you off again, then

stand quiet till you come.
    You, though you climb
higher, farther from me, longer,
    will fall back to me stronger.
Bad penny, pendulum,
    you keep my constant time

to bob in blue July
    where fat goldfinches fly
over the glittering, fecund
    reach of our growing lands.
Once more now, this second,
    I hold you in my hands.

William DeWitt Snodgrass

PAIN FOR A DAUGHTER

Blind with love, my daughter
has cried nightly for horses,
those long-necked marchers and churners
that she has mastered, any and all,
reining them in like a circus hand—
the excitable muscles and the ripe neck—
tending, this summer, a pony and a foal.
She who is too squeamish to pull
a thorn from the dog's paw
watched her pony blossom with distemper,
the underside of the jaw swelling
like an enormous grape.
Gritting her teeth with love,
she drained the boil and scoured it
with hydrogen peroxide until pus
ran like milk on the barn floor.

Blind with loss all winter,
in dungarees, a ski jacket, and a hard hat,
she visits the neighbors' stable,
our acreage not zoned for barns,
they who own the flaming horses
and the swan-whipped thoroughbred
that she tugs at and cajoles,
thinking it will burn like a furnace
under her small-hipped English seat.

Blind with pain, she limps home.
The thoroughbred has stood on her foot.
He rested there like a building.
He grew into her foot until they were one.
The marks of the horseshoe printed
into her flesh, the tips of her toes
ripped off like pieces of leather,
three toenails swirled like shells
and left to float in blood in her riding boot.

Blind with fear, she sits on the toilet,
her foot balanced over the washbasin,
her father, hydrogen peroxide in hand,
performing the rites of the cleansing.
She bites on a towel, sucked in breath,
sucked in and arched against the pain,
her eyes glancing off me where
I stand at the door, eyes locked
on the ceiling, eyes of a stranger,
and then she cries . . .
Oh, my God, help me!
Where a child would have cried *Mama!*
Where a child would have believed *Mama!*
She bit the towel and called on God,
and I saw her life stretch out . . .
I saw her torn in childbirth,
and I saw her, at that moment,
in her own death, and I knew that she
knew.

Anne Sexton

THE ADVERSARY

Mothers are hardest to forgive.
Life is the fruit they long to hand you,
Ripe on a plate. And while you live,
Relentlessly they understand you.

Phyllis McGinley

FIRST LESSON

The thing to remember about fathers is, they're men.
A girl has to keep it in mind.
They are dragon-seekers, bent on improbable rescues.
Scratch any father, you find
Someone chock-full of qualms and romantic terrors,
Believing change is a threat—
Like your first shoes with heels on, like your first bicycle
It took such months to get.

Walk in strange woods, they warn you about the snakes there.
Climb, and they fear you'll fall.
Books, angular boys, or swimming in deep water—
Fathers mistrust them all.
Men are the worriers. It is difficult for them
To learn what they must learn:
How you have a journey to take and very likely,
For a while, will not return.

Phyllis McGinley

AUNT HELEN

Miss Helen Slingsby was my maiden aunt,
And lived in a small house near a fashionable square
Cared for by servants to the number of four.
Now when she died there was silence in heaven
And silence at her end of the street.
The shutters were drawn and the undertaker wiped his feet—
He was aware that this sort of thing had occurred before.
The dogs were handsomely provided for,
But shortly afterwards the parrot died too.
The Dresden clock continued ticking on the mantel-piece,
And the footman sat upon the dining-table
Holding the second housemaid on his knees—
Who had always been so careful while her mistress lived.

T. S. *Eliot*

THE UNEMPLOYED BLACKSMITH

My grandfather was an unemployed blacksmith
when there were working horses
with great shaggy hooves
that rang on stone
as the tidal hay rose in the loft.

He had big wrists
and changed to his winter underwear
while the neighbor kids laughed at the window.
He spat the seeds of Mail Pouch
into the bushes, where they lay
like prune pits.

He was gentle and bald.
I trimmed the coarse gray hair
from his ears, and the barber
paid him not to be shaved.

My father's father, I think,
my grandfather, the long issue,
my eldest eleven.

When I went to the army,
he kissed my face. He died
when I was studying the machinegun.

Mail Pouch signs flake from the barns,
in a world of show horses,
horseshoe-playing firemen,
and grandchildren, standing far back
from the great, twitching flanks
of Percherons.

My grandfather was an unemployed blacksmith
but an employed man.

John Woods

POEM IN PROSE

This poem is for my wife
I have made it plainly and honestly
The mark is on it
Like the burl on the knife

I have not made it for praise
She has no more need for praise
Than summer has
Or the bright days

In all that becomes a woman
Her words and her ways are beautiful
Love's lovely duty
The well-swept room

Wherever she is there is sun
And time and a sweet air
Peace is there
Work done

There are always curtains and flowers
And candles and baked bread
And a cloth spread
And a clean house

Her voice when she sings is a voice
At dawn by a freshening sea
Where the wave leaps in the
Wind and rejoices

Wherever she is it is now
It is here where the apples are
Here in the stars
In the quick hour

The greatest and richest good—
My own life to live in—
This she has given me
If giver could

Archibald MacLeish

A
BOUQUET
OF
BALLADS

AS I WALKED OUT
IN THE STREETS OF LAREDO

As I walked out in the streets of Laredo,
As I walked out in Laredo one day,
I spied a poor cowboy wrapped up in white linen,
Wrapped up in white linen as cold as the clay.

"I see by your outfit that you are a cowboy,"
These words he did say as I boldly stepped by.
"Come, sit down beside me and hear my sad story;
I was shot in the breast and I know I must die.

Once in my saddle I used to look handsome,
Once in my saddle I used to look gay.
I first went to drinkin' and then to card playin',
Got shot in the breast, which ended my day.

Let sixteen gamblers come handle my coffin,
Let sixteen girls come carry my pall;
Put bunches of roses all over my coffin,
Put roses to deaden the clods as they fall.

And beat the drums slowly and play the fife lowly,
And play the dead march as you carry me along;
Take me to the prairie and lay the sod o'er me,
For I'm a young cowboy and I know I've done wrong."

We beat the drums slowly and played the fife lowly,
And bitterly wept as we bore him along;
For we all loved our comrade so brave, young and handsome,
We loved the young cowboy although he'd done wrong.

Anonymous

CASEY JONES

Come, all you rounders, if you want to hear
A story 'bout a brave engineer.
Casey Jones was the rounder's name
On a six-eight wheeler, boys, he won his fame.
The caller called Casey at a half past four,
Kissed his wife at the station door,
Mounted to the cabin with his orders in his hand
And he took his farewell trip to the promised land:
 Casey Jones, mounted to the cabin,
 Casey Jones, with his orders in his hand,
 Casey Jones, mounted to the cabin,
 And he took his farewell trip to the promised land.

"Put in your water and shovel in your coal,
Put your head out the window, watch them drivers roll,
I'll run her till she leaves the rail
'Cause I'm eight hours late with the western mail."
He looked at his watch and his watch was slow,
He looked at the water and the water was low,
He turned to the fireman and then he said,
"We're goin' to reach Frisco but we'll all be dead:"
 Casey Jones, goin' to reach Frisco,
 Casey Jones, but we'll all be dead,
 Casey Jones, goin' to reach Frisco,
 "We're goin' to reach Frisco, but we'll all be dead."

Casey pulled up that Reno Hill,
He tooted for the crossing with an awful shrill,
The switchman knew by the engine's moan
That the man at the throttle was Casey Jones.
He pulled up within two miles of the place
Number Four stared him right in the face,
He turned to the fireman, said, "Boy, you better jump,
'Cause there's two locomotives that's a-goin' to bump:"

> *Casey Jones, two locomotives,*
> *Casey Jones, that's a-goin' to bump,*
> *Casey Jones, two locomotives,*
> *"There's two locomotives that's a-goin' to bump."*

Casey said just before he died,
"There's two more roads that I'd like to ride."
The fireman said what could they be?
"The Southern Pacific and the Santa Fe."
Mrs. Casey sat on her bed a-sighin',
Just received a message that Casey was dyin'.
Said, "Go to bed, children, and hush your cryin',
'Cause you got another papa on the Salt Lake Line:"

> *Mrs. Casey Jones, got another papa,*
> *Mrs. Casey Jones, on that Salt Lake Line,*
> *Mrs. Casey Jones, got another papa,*
> *"And you've got another papa on the Salt Lake Line."*

Anonymous

THE BALLAD OF FATHER GILLIGAN

The old priest Peter Gilligan
Was weary night and day;
For half his flock were in their beds,
Or under green sods lay.

Once, while he nodded on a chair,
At the moth-hour of eve,
Another poor man sent for him,
And he began to grieve.

'I have no rest, nor joy, nor peace,
For people die and die';
And after cried he, 'God forgive!
My body spake, not I!'

He knelt, and leaning on the chair
He prayed and fell asleep;
And the moth-hour went from the fields,
And stars began to peep.

They slowly into millions grew,
And leaves shook in the wind;
And God covered the world with shade,
And whispered to mankind.

Upon the time of sparrow-chirp
When moths came once more,
The old priest Peter Gilligan
Stood upright on the floor.

'Mavrone, mavrone! the man has died
While I slept on the chair';
He roused his horse out of its sleep,
And rode with little care.

He rode now as he never rode,
By rocky lane and fen;
The sick man's wife opened the door:
'Father! you come again!'

'And is the poor man dead?' he cried.
'He died an hour ago.'
The old priest Peter Gilligan
In grief swayed to and fro.

'When you were gone, he turned and died
As merry as a bird.'
The old priest Peter Gilligan
He knelt him at that word.

'He Who hath made the night of stars
For souls who tire and bleed,
Sent one of His great angels down
To help me in my need.

'He Who is wrapped in purple robes,
With planets in His care,
Had pity on the least of things
Asleep upon a chair.'

William Butler Yeats

SPANISH JOHNNY

The old West, the old time,
    The old wind singing through
The red, red grass a thousand miles—
    And, Spanish Johnny, you!
He'd sit beside the water ditch
    When all his herd was in,
And never mind a child, but sing
    To his mandolin.

The big stars, the blue night,
    The moon-enchanted lane:
The olive man who never spoke
    But sang the songs of Spain.
His speech with men was wicked,
    To hear it was a sin;
But those were golden things he said
    To his mandolin.

The gold song, the gold stars,
    The world so golden then:
And the hand so tender to a child
    Had killed so many men.
He died a hard death long ago
    Before the Road came in—
The night before he swung, he sang
    To his mandolin.

Willa Cather

JESSE JAMES

It was on a Wednesday night, the moon was shining bright,
    They robbed the Glendale train.
And the people they did say, for many miles away,
    'Twas the outlaws Frank and Jesse James.

    Jesse had a wife to mourn all her life,
        The children they are brave.
    'Twas a dirty little coward shot Mister Howard,
        And laid Jesse James in his grave.

It was Robert Ford, the dirty little coward,
    I wonder how he does feel,
For he ate of Jesse's bread and he slept in Jesse's bed,
    Then he laid Jesse James in his grave.

It was his brother Frank that robbed the Gallatin bank,
    And carried the money from the town.
It was in this very place that they had a little race,
    For they shot Captain Sheets to the ground.

They went to the crossing not very far from there,
    And there they did the same;
And the agent on his knees he delivered up the keys
  To the outlaws Frank and Jesse James.

It was on a Saturday night, Jesse was at home
    Talking to his family brave,
When the thief and the coward, little Robert Ford,
    Laid Jesse James in his grave.

How people held their breath when they heard of Jesse's
        death,
    And wondered how he ever came to die.
'Twas one of the gang, dirty Robert Ford,
    That shot Jesse James on the sly.

Jesse went to his rest with his hand on his breast.
    The devil will be upon his knee.
He was born one day in the county of Clay,
    And came from a solitary race.

Anonymous

THE WRAGGLE TAGGLE GYPSIES

There were three gypsies a-come to my door,
    And downstairs ran this lady, O.
One sang high and another sang low,
    And the other sang "Bonnie, Bonnie Biscay, O."

Then she pulled off her silken gown,
    And put on hose of leather, O.
With the ragged, ragged rags about her door
    She's off with the wraggle taggle gypsies, O.

'Twas late last night when my lord came home,
    Inquiring for his lady, O.
The servants said on every hand,
    "She's gone with the wraggle taggle gypsies, O."

"Oh, saddle for me my milk-white steed,
    Oh, saddle for me my pony, O,
That I may ride and seek my bride
    Who's gone with the wraggle taggle gypsies, O."

Oh, he rode high and he rode low,
    He rode through woods and copses, O,
Until he came to an open field,
    And there he espied his lady, O.

"What makes you leave your house and lands?
    What makes you leave your money, O?
What makes you leave your new-wedded lord
    To go with the wraggle taggle gypsies, O?"

"What care I for my house and lands?
    What care I for my money, O?
What care I for my new-wedded lord?
    I'm off with the wraggle taggle gypsies, O."

"Last night you slept on a goose-feather bed,
    With the sheet turned down so bravely, O.
Tonight you will sleep in the cold, open field,
    Along with the wraggle taggle gypsies, O."

"What care I for your goose-feather bed,
    With the sheet turned down so bravely, O?
For tonight I shall sleep in a cold, open field,
    Along with the wraggle taggle gypsies, O."

Anonymous

OH! DEAR, WHAT CAN THE MATTER BE?

Oh! dear, what can the matter be?
    Dear! dear! What can the matter be?
Oh! dear, what can the matter be?
    Johnny's so long at the fair.

He promised he'd buy me a beautiful fairing,
A gay bit of lace that the lassies are wearing,
He promised he'd bring me a bunch of blue ribbons
To tie up my bonny brown hair.

Oh! dear, what can the matter be?
    Dear! dear! What can the matter be?
Oh! dear, what can the matter be?
    Johnny's so long at the fair.

He promised he'd buy me a basket of posies,
A garland of lilies, a wreath of red roses,
A little straw hat to set off the blue ribbons
That tie up my bonny brown hair.

Anonymous

SIMPLE
NONSENSE

SONG OF THE POP-BOTTLERS

Pop bottles pop-bottles
    In pop shops;
The pop-bottles Pop bottles
    Poor Pop drops.

When Pop drops pop-bottles,
    Pop-bottles plop!
Pop-bottle-tops topple!
    Pop mops slop!

Stop! Pop'll drop bottle!
    Stop, Pop, stop!
When Pop bottles pop-bottles,
    Pop-bottles pop!

Morris Bishop

SOLILIQUY OF A TORTOISE
ON REVISITING
THE LETTUCE BEDS
AFTER AN INTERVAL OF ONE HOUR
WHILE SUPPOSED
TO BE
SLEEPING
IN A CLUMP
OF BLUE HOLLYHOCKS

One Cannot have enough
Of this delicious stuff!

E. V. Rieu

THE OCTOPUS

Tell me, O Octopus, I begs,
Is those things arms, or is they legs?
I marvel at thee, Octopus;
If I were thou, I'd call me Us.

Ogden Nash

ANCIENT HISTORY

I hope the old Romans
Had painful abdomens.

I hope that the Greeks
Had toothache for weeks.

I hope the Egyptians
Had chronic conniptions.

I hope that the Arabs
Were bitten by scarabs.

I hope that the Vandals
Had thorns in their sandals.

I hope that the Persians
Had gout in all versions.

I hope that the Medes
Were kicked by their steeds.

They started the fuss
And left it to us!

Arthur Guiterman

LITTLE WILLIE

Little Willie from his mirror
    Licked the mercury right off,
Thinking, in his childish error,
    It would cure the whooping cough.
At the funeral his mother
    Smartly said to Mrs. Brown:
" 'Twas a chilly day for Willie
When the mercury went down."

Anonymous

THE SNIFFLE

In spite of her sniffle,
Isabel's chiffle.
Some girls with a sniffle
Would be weepy and tiffle;
They would look awful,
Like a rained-on waffle,
But Isabel's chiffle
In spite of her sniffle.
Her nose is more red
With a cold in her head,
But then, to be sure,
Her eyes are bluer.
Some girls with a snuffle,
Their tempers are uffle,
But when Isabel's snivelly
She's snivelly civilly,
And when she is snuffly
She's perfectly luffly.

Ogden Nash

THE TUTOR

A tutor who tooted a flute,
Tried to teach two young tooters to toot.
 Said the two to the tutor,
 "Is it harder to toot, or
To tutor two tooters to toot?"

Carolyn Wells

AS I WAS LAYING ON THE GREEN

As I was laying on the green,
A small English book I seen.
Carlyle's *Essay on Burns* was the edition,
So I left it laying in the same position.

Anonymous

THE SONG OF THE JELLICLES

Jellicle Cats come out to-night,
Jellicle Cats come one come all:
The Jellicle Moon is shining bright—
Jellicles come to the Jellicle Ball.

Jellicle Cats are black and white,
Jellicle Cats are rather small;
Jellicle Cats are merry and bright,
And pleasant to hear when they caterwaul.
Jellicle Cats have cheerful faces,
Jellicle Cats have bright black eyes;
They like to practise their airs and graces
And wait for the Jellicle Moon to rise.

Jellicle Cats develop slowly,
Jellicle Cats are not too big;
Jellicle Cats are roly-poly,
They know how to dance a gavotte and a jig.
Until the Jellicle Moon appears
They make their toilette and take their repose:
Jellicles wash behind their ears,
Jellicles dry between their toes.

Jellicle Cats are white and black,
Jellicle Cats are of moderate size;
Jellicles jump like a jumping-jack,
Jellicle Cats have moonlit eyes.

They're quiet enough in the morning hours,
They're quiet enough in the afternoon,
Reserving their terpsichorean powers
To dance by the light of the Jellicle Moon.

Jellicle Cats are black and white,
Jellicle Cats (as I said) are small;
If it happens to be a stormy night
They will practise a caper or two in the hall.
If it happens the sun is shining bright
You would say they had nothing to do at all:
They are resting and saving themselves to be right
For the Jellicle Moon and the Jellicle Ball.

T. S. Eliot

THE FLY AND THE FLEA

A flea and a fly in a flue
Were imprisoned, so what could they do?
    Said the fly, "Let us flee,"
    Said the flea, "Let us fly,"
So they flew through a flaw in the flue.

Anonymous

AUNT ELIZA

In the drinking-well
    Which the plumber built her,
Aunt Eliza fell . . . .
    . . . We must buy a filter.

Harry Graham

EDOUARD

A bugler named Dougal MacDougal
Found ingenious ways to be frugal.
He learned how to sneeze
In various keys,
Thus saving the price of a bugle.

Ogden Nash

INDEX

INDEX